THE
FAST
TRACK
TO
WAKING
UP

The Fast Track To Waking Up

Copyright © Linda Penny, 2022

First Edition

ISBN (paperback) [978-1-914447-55-6]

ISBN (eBook) [978-1-914447-56-3]

Prepared by TGH International Ltd.

www.TGHBooks.com

FAST TRACK TO WAKING UP

RAISE YOUR CONSCIOUSNESS IN 11 SIMPLE STEPS

Anara

THE WAKE UP ARTIST

Dedication

This book is dedicated to my amazing grandchildren, Jackson and Zoe, who give me so much joy and remind me constantly of the true meaning of unconditional love. And to my son, Chris, who has believed in me always and loved and supported me in all my endeavours.

I wish to acknowledge all the teachers, friends, and experiences that appeared in my life to show me my true authentic self.
Not always easy, but always necessary.

I also wish to thank my dear friend, Alex, who introduced me to Sean at TGH Books. She believed in me from many years ago when I first started the book and has been a big part of my journey.

And of course, I am grateful to all my many clients and students who inspired this book by asking me so many questions. I hope this answers some of them for you.

Through the work that I do, raising our vibration has been a mission of mine for many years. It is essential for us to create a new harmonious world. I trust that this little handbook will offer all those souls who are looking for an easier way to navigate their lives, a way to find more peace, love and joy in every day.

I love you all.

It's time to Wake Up...

Contents

Introduction

Time to Wake Up!

Join me on **The Fast Track to Waking Up.** It's a great ride. If you participate and use the tools I give you, you'll find your life will change for the better. You will open up a part of yourself that is dormant and your true self will emerge, complete with the creativity you never knew you had. You'll find ways to access that part of you that is divine – your divine self that knew you were divine when you chose to come here. You made the necessary plans and then forgot.

Ready?

Well, let's start ...

There may be many reasons why you are reading this.

Hope for a happier future? Regret and a desire to change? Curiosity? Cynicism?

Whatever the reasons, I hope that this little handbook will reach not just those who are open to a holistic approach to life, but also those whose beliefs are more empirical. Let me show you how to WAKE UP with easy steps that can change your life.

11 Steps to Change Your Life

A few pages further on, you'll find 11 steps that can change your life. Since this is *The Fast Track to Waking Up*, feel free to jump directly to those steps.

Implement them.

They're not difficult. In fact, they may be rather obvious. You may wonder why you haven't followed them before.

Try them.

Feel the change in your life and your being. That feeling will be the empirical evidence that you are on the fast track.

Why Wake Up at All?

I'm not the first person to realize that I spent much of my life asleep at the wheel. As I went through life, it sent me a series of wake-up calls and each time, I thought I responded to the call, but then I'd get another and that would make me realize that I still wasn't fully awake. And I believe that's one of the constants of life – that we will get those wake-up calls and, if we don't respond, we'll keep getting them until we finally do quit sleeping on the job... the job of living.

We get those wake-up calls because our true self wants to be awake and alive: to enjoy the day, to seize the opportunities for happiness and fulfilment, to be energized and excited about our lives.

Our True Self Wants to Live, but Sometimes the Mind Gets in the Way

The Fast Track to Waking Up puts you in control of your own life because many of us are not in control. We have been subjected to society's agendas, beliefs and systems and consequently locked into our amazing minds are fears and doubts, memories, learned behaviours and survival techniques, which might have once worked but now inhibit us.

Everything here is based on the belief that you are in charge of your life and your attitudes. Your thoughts are yours – or can be. At the deepest levels, no matter what your circumstances, each moment you live is uniquely yours. You have the power to find the positive within it. In fact, you have the power to open yourself up to life, to allow it to fill you, to find the joy and laughter.

It's very hard to be miserable when you're laughing.

Before we start, it will make all the difference in the world if you firstly understand two words: Awareness & Consciousness – they are intrinsically linked.

By *raising* your awareness, you *raise* your consciousness. You start to see life, and all the circumstances and situations in a different perspective. You may start to realize that we are, in fact, multidimensional beings.

Perspective? It changes slowly, a little at a time so that sometimes it's hardly noticeable, but it *is* happening. You begin to see yourself and the life you have created from a different viewpoint; a healthier, happier viewpoint. As your awareness rises and you become more conscious of who you *really* are, you begin to realize you have choices.

You can *choose* to be happy, or you can *choose* to be miserable.

Which one do you choose?

And who am I?

Just think of me as the *Wake-Up Artist.*

Awareness & Consciousness

These two words have become part of our vocabulary but I'm not sure that we really understand their meaning.

What do these words mean to me?

Let's start with **AWARENESS.**

I use the word awareness so much that I hadn't really stopped to look at it's definition. I have to say there are many descriptions and uses for it. You can be aware of a pain in your body, and you can also be aware of your connection to nature. To me, it means noticing what's going on in your life and the world around you. Not just understanding it, but *really* seeing it for the truth that it is.

Awareness is a state of being.

When you're awake, you are aware. When you are asleep, you are not aware.

Awareness is closely linked to your level of consciousness. For example, when you have awareness, you are aware of your own actions, of the reasons behind things and of the bigger picture.

Being aware helps you to have a deeper understanding of what is important in life and what is not.

Being an aware human means that you have a certain understanding of the way the universe works. You have a belief system that suits you, and you definitely don't just sit back and accept everything you are told.

You are aware of how to think, and that awareness allows you to view yourself objectively with a certain level of understanding, both inside and outside of yourself.

What is the 'inside'?

The *inside* is where we go when we meditate or become very quiet. We are then able to look inside of ourselves. This is where we connect with Source, our God-self, our Higher Self, the part of us that is more than we can see. We are then conscious of our connection to all that there is and understand that we are more than flesh and blood. We are aware of our connection to Source, our Higher Self, God, Infinite Intelligence, Universal Energy. However ,we don't judge it – we are just *aware* of it.

There are many levels of awareness and many levels of consciousness. As you become more awake, your awareness grows; it raises your vibration and that in turn raises your level of consciousness. So, the state of consciousness you achieve is directly related to the level of awareness you experience. It is possible to consciously work on raising your vibration and therefore your awareness by 'working' on yourself. You can take responsibility to make the necessary changes that are required to raise your vibration. To come to a place of understanding that you are so much more than what you see in the mirror.

That is what this book is intended to do, to help you on *The Fast Track to Waking Up*.

Once you start this work, you may very well become aware that you are, in fact, a beautiful being of light and that every cell in your body is a thinking cell. That's a biggie, but it's also a fact and has been proven by quantum physicists. Deepak Chopra, many years ago, was one of the first authors to describe in his books that our cells have innate intelligence and deserve respect.

For over 30 years, I have been helping people to raise their vibration, which in turn improves all aspects of themselves - be it their health, emotions, attitude, belief system etc.

As a Kinesiologist and healer, I have the wonderful tool of *Muscle Testing*, which enables me to talk to the innate intelligence of the body. This communication bypasses the brain and gets to the truth of what is going on, the source, if you will, of the issue.

To help you raise your vibration, be aware of what you put in your body. EVERYTHING YOU PUT IN YOUR BODY IS IMPORTANT. This includes your thoughts, so notice what you choose to think.

Take time to be still and meditate.

Ok, now let's look at **CONSCIOUSNESS.**

This word *consciousness* has a plethora of meanings and can be used in many contexts. For instance, you are aware of being conscious or unconscious. The body works unconsciously all the time; you don't consciously have to make your blood circulate, or your digestion system produce the enzymes needed to break down your food, or the glands to produce the hormones you need. However, you are conscious of moving your body to stretch and lift. You are able to consciously decide whether to turn left or right at the end of the street. You make conscious and unconscious decisions all day long.

The consciousness I am referring to is the connection to all that there is... to everything... to God ... to the highest part of ourselves ... to understanding that there is only one energy, and we are all connected.

We are all one.

When we feel our connection to our Oneness, we feel the power of who we really are.

Einstein proved that everything is energy, so we don't have to worry about whether it's real or not – it is! It's being aware of yourself and who you really are. Universal Energy is the essence of everything and is consciousness... you can be aware of this energy and become it if you so choose.

Being in a particular state of consciousness and being aware that you are conscious gives you a wonderful sense of yourself within this Universe. As I said before, the words 'awareness' and 'consciousness' are intrinsically linked and cannot be defined separately.

As their meaning explains, we are all connected to this one energy – some of us are aware of that and have become conscious beings, while others have not... YET. They are still asleep – and that is their choice.

There is no judgment for either awareness or consciousness. It is something that happens to certain individuals at their correct time... or maybe not at all.

Being conscious is a sense of your identity in this vast Universe.

Wake-Up Calls... My Story

I've had a few wake-up calls in my lifetime. I've also had a near-death experience and have seen spirits and angels since I was quite young. These experiences are real to me. I experienced them, therefore, I have no problem in believing that there is more to me and to life than I can see.

I have seen a life after death.

I have had visits to other dimensions.

I am able to communicate with my higher self.

These things are perfectly normal to me, and I have no need to prove them or to persuade others that they indeed happened.

They are *my* experiences as I'm sure you have *yours*.

I will share with you an experience I had when I was 5 or 6 years old.

I lost my mother when I was very young and was sent away to school to be cared for. The first school I was sent to, I hated. I distinctly remember crying in my bed. I was the youngest and sent to bed earlier than everyone else. I was on my own in what seemed like a huge dormitory with rows of metal beds. I felt very alone there. I was taken out of there after a few months (my dad could see how unhappy I was) and put in another boarding school in Broadstairs, UK. I loved it! It was a lovely house with only a few boarders, run by two very jolly big ladies. I remember one who was called Mrs. Johnson, but I can't remember the other one. I was in a dormitory with about eight other girls.

One evening, for some reason or other, I couldn't sleep. Everyone else seemed to be asleep. I was tossing and turning and then, all of a sudden, I had the feeling that there was someone at the end of my bed. I knew it wasn't any of the other girls, and it didn't feel like the teachers. I felt scared, and I remember distinctly hiding under the sheets. I pulled them tight around me.

After a few moments, the fear subsided and I had this amazing feeling of calm and love. It was beautiful. I gently peeped out from under the covers to see a grayish figure at the side of my bed. I didn't feel so scared then. I knew I was safe, just a little shocked. There were, in fact, a number of grayish figures around my bed, all looking at me lovingly. I watched them until they left and then went back to sleep and didn't mention it to anyone. I felt they were looking after me and, from that day on, I always felt I was not alone. I was a part of some other world and belonged somewhere else.

My childhood was spent at school, not in a home environment, and with very little influence or time with my father. This didn't seem to bother me, as I always felt there were 'people' with me all the time. Loving 'people', like the ones I had seen around my bed. In fact, my nickname at school a few years later was "Sputnik," due to the fact that when asked where I came from (meaning which town in England) I would always answer, "I'm not from here. I'm not sure where I am from, but I know I'm not from here. I'm just visiting."

I still think that to this day.

I know this episode was real because I've had other experiences that were similar throughout my life. Once I became aware and conscious, life became so much easier. I gave up any feelings I may have had of being a victim. I became forgiving. I understood that I create my reality by my thoughts and actions and that I have choices all day long.

It's up to me, this life of mine. I'm in charge of it. What a relief!!!! I realized that I'm *in* the world but I'm not *of* it.

That doesn't mean I'm perfect... far from it.

I still have challenges to deal with. I am still improving myself and growing. I still take time to learn and connect with my higher self. I still make mistakes. I know there are still parts of me that have not as yet been born. I have potential that I haven't tapped yet... but that's great! How dull life would be if you had finally become aware, become conscious, and that was it.

What would you do all day – sit on a log?

No. I'm happy to say that I am in service, continually, until I decide to leave. I am no longer ruled by others. I have offered myself to God, the Universe, the Energy, and I am *in* service. I surrender each day to his will, to his love and to his guidance.

I ask each day, *"How can I be of service?"*

Your uniqueness is your greatness.

— Michael beckwith

Don't ask yourself what the world needs. Ask yourself what makes you come alive, and then go do that. Because what the world needs is people who have come alive.

— Harold Thurman Whitman

Chapter 1

Keep It Simple

A simple life is a contented life.

Isn't that what we all want?

Well, yes, ideally. However, when I started my *journey to waking up* I didn't feel that way. In fact, I doubt if many of us actually do have a contented life. The reason why being that I had surrounded myself with so much stuff, noise and things, and given myself so many responsibilities and expectations, that I could hardly ever find a quiet moment to be still and just enjoy being alive.

Do you find that, too? How many times this year have you stopped, for say one hour, and just enjoyed *being*; not doing anything or listening to music, checking your phone or your email, not scrolling through social media or even reading, but just *being*?

Not often, if at all, I hear you say.

I'll make this as simple as possible because life *is* simple.

I soon realized that it was all down to me and that I had made it complicated. I had decided to fill my life full of jobs, friends, activities, expectations and stress etc. and it was up to me to make the changes towards a more contented and happy life. I have learnt that by keeping life simple, we release more energy for experiencing what we really want to do and create a more peaceful, happy and simple environment in which to live.

Stress seems to be the biggest bugbear in our lives today.

Do you think there has always been stress?

Interesting question, isn't it?

I think you'll find that we create more stress in our 'civilized' world than necessary because it has become a habit. It's become a way of being, and we can choose to change that habit by changing the way we function. This step is fundamental. If we re-address how we live, and make the necessary changes, we can alleviate stress and enjoy a stress-free life once again.

KISS – is the buzz word. Keep It Simple, Sweetheart

I remember being given this word at the beginning of my Kinesiology training in England many years ago. It made me laugh, and I loved it; it became a mantra for me for years to come. It is true, we make things so complicated that we exhaust ourselves. We seem to be constantly sorting things out.

But *why*?

How did we get to be in such a muddle and decide to become a hamster on a wheel?

I understand it's quite challenging in our busy world to *keep it simple* because there are numerous responsibilities, choices and decisions to be made all day long. However, by making things easy, by making things *simple*, you can work at your own pace and achieve a lot more.

We all have those voices in our heads that have so many different opinions. The negative ones and the positive ones. The idea is to spend some time calming and clearing the mind with exercise, meditation or any other relaxation method you prefer.

So, here are some suggestions to do just that...

1. Balance Your Brain

One key to a clearer mind, more clarity and increased energy is to integrate both sides of the brain.

Studying kinesiology introduced me to a very simple exercise that is specifically designed to do just that and it's called Cross Crawl. Some of you may be familiar with this practice, as it is used in many areas of health nowadays, as well as being taught in schools such as Brain Gym.

Cross Crawl allows the left hemisphere of the brain to send information to the right side of the body, and vice versa. It is particularly useful when you are feeling tired, and after just a few minutes revitalizes and energizes you.

It couldn't be simpler: just march on the spot. Alternatively, touching each hand to the opposite knee, and continuing the action for as long as is comfortable.

So, give it a go. Each morning, do at least 50 Cross Crawls and see the results!

2. K.I.S.S. – It's extremely simple!!

The way this works is to understand that there are two sides to the brain.

The right side of the brain is our intuitive and creative side; it is fluid, spontaneous, and conceptual and responds without fear or judgment. It absorbs the experience of life without question and lives in present time. It is the part of us that knows we are all connected... that we are *one*.

The left side of our brain is our action side; it is logical, good at math, analytical and ordered. It calculates, observes, judges and is responsible for those voices that keep reminding us of all those things we need to do. So yes, the *chitter-chatter* in our heads is from the left brain.

In this day and age, in the kind of society we have created, the left side is overworked most of the time. We don't spend much time experiencing the right side at all. Ideally, we need to have our left and right brain working in balance and harmony, so that we have more clarity and so that our decision-making process is based on total input from *both* sides of the brain.

By doing this exercise regularly, you will see lots of benefits, including improving your memory, achieving clearer thinking, reducing stress, balancing your emotions, and of course, balancing the right and left brain.

3. Calming the Mind

Meditation is the easiest and most effective way of calming your mind because *it's simple!*

I know it sounds difficult and, *believe me,* I thought it was too before I started doing it. There are so many people telling you to do meditation in a certain way that it becomes quite overwhelming. However, meditation can bring you a wonderful feeling of peace once you have mastered it.

I have meditated for many years without instruction. I simply get comfortable, close my eyes, and put my attention on my breathing. When I first started, I found it helpful to use a guided meditation or have gentle music on in the background. In fact, I still very often use music to give me something to focus on and enjoy the calmness it brings. Before too long, I don't even hear my breathing as I am far away from my everyday world. I go to the place where we are all connected as one energy.

Just sitting quietly and being still has huge rewards.

Try it: close your eyes, be still and focus your attention on your breathing. Be patient with yourself when you start meditation. It may take many months before the chitter-chatter stops and you find that peaceful, quiet place. As thoughts come to you, observe them and let them pass. The trick is not to attach to them, just let them go.

Become the *Objective Observer*.

Find time for yourself, something most people find very difficult.

Start with just a few minutes and build up slowly to 10 minutes, then after a few days or even weeks, move to 20 minutes. Give yourself permission to take half an hour out of your day just for you. (This is the hard part of meditation, spending time by yourself doing nothing).

I can tell you from my own experience that meditation takes away the everyday feelings of stress and gives me more clarity and a sense of purpose. I often come out of meditation knowing exactly what needs to be done. Which one of my many jobs on the to-do-list needs my attention. Often, it's not the one I was intending to do, however once I have tackled that particular job, I find the rest seems to disappear.

There is so much more to you than you realize. There is a whole other part of you that you probably haven't been aware of. It's the part of the trinity of Mind-Body-

Spirit that has been asleep. You may have spotted it once in a while and chosen to ignore it, but it's there. The whole of you, the sum of all the parts that makes up the wonderful being that you are.

4. Simple Thoughts

To find that place of peace, we need to simplify our thoughts.

Remember the phrase *short and sweet?*

Well, that can apply to your thoughts. Think short and simple thoughts, one at a time.

When your thoughts start to overwhelm you or make you anxious, take a breath and distract yourself (maybe go for a walk). It's important that you make some space between your thoughts and maybe write them down so you can clearly see what is actually going on in your head.

When you're talking, slow down your speech and really listen to what you are saying. An idea I've used which I think is great fun is to record yourself talking. It's fascinating to hear yourself because you'll be surprised by how often you repeat yourself or say *um* and *ah*. Each person listening to themselves will hear things they probably didn't know, and even solve their problems, all by talking it over with themselves!

I've been doing this for many years. Having lived alone for a long time, I have become my best friend, and when I have a decision to make or a problem to solve, I often sit at my dressing table in front of the mirror and have a good old chat with myself. I find it works wonders and I feel much clearer at the end of it. So much better than letting those thoughts go round and round inside your head. Get them out either by talking or writing them down, you'll definitely feel the benefit.

Remember that *we* choose our thoughts.

No one tells us what to think, although society has a bloody good go by way of the media and advertising. Don't buy into the fear of society... I don't read the papers, have a television or watch the news.

I can hear you saying, *"WHAT?"*

Yes, you heard me...give up on the media.

It will give you so much less to think about and reduce your levels of stress – it's amazingly freeing!

Of course, I understand you want to know what's going on in the world, and believe me, you will. You can get the headlines sent to you by email or text and probably hear via social media but this way you can choose the subjects you want to know about and ignore the rest.

The less thoughts you put in your mind, especially negative or fearful ones, the more energy and clarity you will have.

So, keep it simple and don't get caught up in the news. Most of it is none of your business anyway. I mean, are you *really* interested in what celebrities are doing?

> *Once you are feeling better, have more energy and can think clearer, your whole life will improve.*

5. Go For a Walk

Something else I find that clears the mind is to go for a walk, regularly, first thing in the morning if possible. You may not feel like it when you wake up, but if you are able (and fit enough) give it a try early in the morning. A brisk walk upon rising brings fresh air and oxygen to your brain and body, plus the act of walking connects your right and left brain, and you already know how valuable that is.

You will find that you have more energy for the rest of the day.

6. Keep it Simple at Home

Your home is an extension of you. Your energy resides there, so it's very important that you feel happy and relaxed when you are at home. It helps immensely if it is tidy, clean and in order and not full of unwanted items and papers shoved in drawers.

The rudimentary requirement of *Feng Shui* is an ancient Chinese belief that the way your house is built or the way that you arrange objects affects your success, health and happiness. The idea is to clear out clutter from your life, not just from your home but from your mind and body, as well as your environment. By clearing your home, you clear your mind, which in turn clears your emotions and you find that you are much more peaceful.

Can you find what you need in your home when you need it? Can you find your important papers like birth certificate, passport, etc. without searching and getting stressed? Is your address book up to date? Do you have a record of important family birthdays etc? Are your clothes sorted so that you can make easy decisions each day about what to wear?

These seem like obvious questions but, in fact, most people would answer no to all three.

The first step is to decide to sort out your cupboards and closets. You can do this by making a special place for important papers and things like scissors, scotch tape, first-aid supplies and keys. By clearing away old papers and cleaning out drawers, when you need something, you will know automatically where it is and you won't have to stress about it (of course, this means that you have *to put them away* after use). Most of all, you will see what you are holding on to that you really don't need.

What possessions are you attached to that are taking all your energy?

We've been trained to be consumers and to get into debt so let's decide to change that and only purchase what we need and can afford.

Take your time doing all of this, there is no rush. Take one step at a time.

Remember. Keep it simple.

I did this exercise myself quite a few years ago, and was doing really well until I got to my books. I found that when it came to clearing out my book collection it was *really* difficult. I was so attached to all my books that the idea of getting rid of any of them seemed impossible. I loved them all so much and the idea of being without even one of them was just not in my consciousness. It actually amazed me how emotional I became at the idea of giving my books away.

I mentioned this in one of my psychic development classes that I was attending at the time. It was explained to me that the amount of emotional energy I was using to keep those books on the shelves was enormous. Not only was I energetically attached to over 500 books, but as long as they were sitting on my shelf (having already been read many years previously) I was denying other people the wonderful experience I had when I first read them.

That made so much sense to me.

Of course, if I give them away, other people can enjoy them, which will make me feel good which will free up my energy and also make space for something new to come in.

So, I went home and over the next few weeks managed to quite happily cull my book collection. I gave over 200 books away to friends, students, clients and charity shops. I gave them away lovingly. In fact, I thoroughly enjoyed giving them away and got a real kick out of it. I knew how much other people would enjoy them as I had, and I knew that if I really needed to read any of the again, I could go to the library or if need be, buy it again.

I felt so much lighter, and, in turn, had more energy.

It's funny though, as much as I miss some of my books, I seem to have acquired a whole bunch more new ones that have filled my heart all over again. However, I no longer have the same desperate attachment to them, which leaves me feeling freer. I have simplified my life by not being attached to my favorite possessions.

You can cull your belongings with the knowledge that you are simplifying your life and therefore making it less stressful and easier... *much* easier.

7. Planning Your Day

Now, here is something you can start to do right away and see the results immediately; prioritize.

Make a list of all the things you need to do each day and prioritize the ones that you know you have to take care of. The ones that are really important, even if they happen to be the ones you least like doing. Do this when you go to bed so that you can clear your mind and know you won't forget anything overnight, as it's on the list for you to see in the morning.

It helps you sleep better, too.

At the bottom of the page, make another list of the ones that are left and put them under the heading of:

*THINGS I WANT THE UNIVERSE
TO TAKE CARE OF FOR ME*

You'll be surprised how many of those get taken care of or just seem to disappear as though they never existed.

Try it, it's quite amazing!

Another very important factor to keeping it simple is to Let Go and Surrender. Let go of all those feelings and thoughts of resentment, anger, guilt, fear or other negative feelings. Most of us have some negative emotions shoved away inside of us somewhere. Check in and see if you are holding any negative thoughts of any kind, and if you are it's time to let them go and release them. Believe me, they are holding you back and complicating your life.

There are a number of ways to do this. A very simple and effective one is by using your intention to surrender those feelings through writing.

It works brilliantly and efficiently.

Let me explain...

8. Write a letter

Dear God/Source/Universe/Higher Self

I ask you please to clear my mind of anger, hate, resentment (whatever the emotion is) towards (insert name, or just in general).

I surrender these feelings to you and know they will be replaced with positive feeling of love, forgiveness, compassion, joy and honesty.

My intention is to no longer hold on to these negative emotions, but to release them and in so doing release myself from the pain and unhappiness that they produce.

My intention is to live a life full of love and joy. To forgive myself and everyone I have encountered in my life.

And so it is.

This little exercise is incredibly powerful as many *simple* things are. You can write letters for each negative situation, feeling or emotion that you have or feel, and watch it melt away with very little effort. The whole idea of using these simple exercises to simplify your life is to find time for you. Time to walk, time to enjoy your food, time to watch the sunset, time with friends and family, time alone, time to laugh and have fun, time to connect with the Universe... time to just *be*.

By bringing these simple suggestions into your life, you will make time for yourself... just watch what happens.

Chapter 2

Be Grateful

This is one of the most powerful words in our vocabulary. Truly, this word *gratitude*, when used honestly and regularly, will change your life.

I'm not kidding.

I started being grateful at a time in my life where everything was going wrong and when my life was a mess. I had a lot of lack; lack of enthusiasm, lack of joy, lack of money, lack of self-worth... just lack in general.

It was bringing me down and making me miserable.

At the time, a friend of mine suggested that I started focusing on all the things I was grateful for. She told me to look around and realize how lucky I am compared to many others. That changed my perception.

I started by being grateful for my eyesight, for my two arms and two legs, for my hearing, and the fact that I could walk and talk and function in the world. That soon progressed to looking around and being grateful for my bed, for my pillow, for my fridge, for my apartment, for my bathtub (I love baths), for my car and, of course, for my family and friends.

In fact, once I got going, I couldn't stop.

I found so many things to be grateful for that I began to realize how lucky I was and forgot to focus on what I didn't have.

I was grateful for my intelligence, my common sense, my ability to type and use a computer, my library of books that gave me a vast array of interesting and fascinating knowledge.

In fact, I needed to use that knowledge.

I had become depressed, like many of us do, as life was not going the way I had expected. But now, looking at all I was grateful for, I came to the understanding that I had a choice, that we have choices, every day, so I started making *new* choices that would shape my future forever.

I started a Gratitude Journal and would write a minimum of 10 things I was grateful for each morning before I got out of bed. This is a technique that I have given to hundreds of clients over the years. The best example was from a young boy of about six years old.

His mother had brought him to me as he was suffering from depression. He didn't want to go to school, he just wanted to stay in his room alone. I suggested while he was in there that he start a *Gratitude Diary* and write down five things he was grateful for each day.

Well, it wasn't long before I got a call from his mother saying he wanted to talk to me. He was so excited to tell me that he could do almost 20 'gratefuls' every day. In fact, he had been including more each day as a game. Now he was up to 20, and I realized it had become a competition to see how many he could come up with. I told him that I was thrilled that he could play this game so well, and as far as I knew he was the winner so far. This made him very happy (something he hadn't been for a while) and in general his state of mind started to improve daily.

The next time I saw him for a treatment he bounced in my office with a big smile.

"I can do 25 now. Want to hear?"

"Yes, let's hear them", I said.

Practicing gratitude helps to open our hearts and feel love, it helps you appreciate everything in your life and nudges you to say thank you more often, to show appreciation of others.

That's what being grateful does – it shifts your perception of life. Things don't look quite so terrible as they did. No matter how hard things get, there is always something to be grateful for.

Try it for yourself... *what have you got to lose?*

Being grateful is a feeling of appreciation. There is a subtle difference. We can *feel* gratitude and *show* appreciation. This applies to many areas of our life. We can be grateful for our job, and show appreciation by doing it well, or we can be grateful for our body and our home and show appreciation by taking care of them.

If you come from a place of gratitude, you will see how your life changes. Get yourself a super brand-new colorful journal, one that you like the look of, and start writing down 5–10 gratitudes a day, first thing in the morning, and see what happens. We forget how much we do have, how many wonderful people are in our lives. How we are able to see, breathe, walk, etc.

Focusing on gratitude changes your mindset and allows for 'good feelings' to come to the surface, and from these good feelings come wonderful experiences.

Once I started doing this, I found that I was grateful all day for so many things. I make a point now of noticing the wonderful moments in life when I feel happy, when my life flows easily and effortlessly, and I'm grateful for all those precious moments.

Use this technique regularly to improve the quality of your life. Enjoy playing the Gratitude Game!

When I started counting my blessings, my whole life turned around.

— Willie Nelson

Chapter 3

Think Big

I t might sound a little strange to *'think big'* but when you open your mind and heart you will allow your thinking to *expand* and consequently start to 'think big'.

Thinking Big means mastering the ability to use your imagination and visualization to dream and believe you can achieve anything you desire (well, almost anything). It's about being open-minded, positive, creative and seeing opportunity in the big picture. Thinking Big means losing the limitations in your thoughts. We often limit our thinking as we don't necessarily believe we deserve more than we have, or are worthy of the changes we would like to see, and feel they are too far away from us, out of our reach.

It starts with a feeling...

Allow yourself to feel; feel love, compassion, joy and happiness on a regular basis. The more you feel good about yourself, in fact, *love* yourself, the more you begin to realize that you deserve the very best in life, and that you have the ability to change your existing situation to something that suits you better.

It's not always easy and that old chestnut *fear* often gets in the way.

Don't let that stop you.

You can choose to live in fear, or you can choose to live in love...but you can't live in both. We see fear as the opposite of love in the world of consciousness.

Allow yourself to think BIG.

Big ideas, big solutions, big desires and big goals.

Don't limit yourself.

By doing this you will see life with a different perspective and have a better understanding of the Universe and your place in it. We have all been programmed to think we are small and insignificant, and so many of us grew up with low self-esteem.

A lot of us still have it!

The truth is, we were programmed by society, news, school, parents, religion, TV, etc. to rely on some outer source for confirmation of who we are. We weren't taught to rely on our instincts, our intuition or 'gut feelings'. We became used to going outside of ourselves to be validated, by the teachers, preachers, parents, etc. It's those parts of ourselves that have become dormant due to lack of use. You use your gut feeling as a guide, so that you know when something feels right or wrong.

In order to make your new beliefs a reality, you can use your imagination. You can replace old beliefs with new and exciting ones that suit your life much better with the help of your imagination. You change your perspective when you change your belief system.

The bottom line (and I'm a bottom line person) is that you are amazing... huge... fantastic and capable of so much more than you realize.

We are all capable of so much more than we realize if we changed our belief system.

There are many ways to expand your mind and get out of your 'little me' mindset.

The following are a few suggestions I have used myself and with clients in the past and had great results.

Emotional Freedom Technique (EFT), often referred to as tapping.

Have you heard of tapping?

By tapping various points on the side of the hand, the face, head and body you access 'energy points' called *meridians* and by stimulating these points, you release the various emotions that are stuck there, allowing you to clear pain, old beliefs and programs.

Negative emotions and high stress levels are detrimental to the body, and EFT is a brilliant, easy and effective way of clearing those stressors, allowing you to feel bigger, lighter and more in control of your life.

I have been tapping with Brad Yates online for many years. He is an exceptionally nice guy and offers a plethora of videos for clearing all kinds of emotional issues from procrastination to allowing yourself to have a great day.

Use Your Imagination

We have this amazing tool, our imagination, but how often do we really use the power of our imagination to its full potential?

I know that many athletes use their imagination to see themselves winning their particular sport, often with excellent results.

When you have a problem to solve or an idea that is festering, try scheduling some thinking time and use your imagination and get away from your surroundings for a while. I find a walk works wonders to clear my mind after sitting at the computer. There's something about getting outside and physically moving that helps me to relax and clear my mind.

I also use my imagination by thinking about how I would like to see certain situations pan out. I imagine the final outcome and see it all come together effortlessly. Don't focus on *how* it will all work out, focus on the outcome as you wish to see it. It's not always a one-time thing, and often requires that you use your imagination on a daily basis so that you can practice the art.

You can give birth to new possibilities through your ability to reach into the future and let go of the past.

When was the last time you wrote down all the things you would like to achieve in your life? Did you ever do that?

Did you ever think of doing that?

Well, I have this great idea for you. Try it. I've used it myself and given it to many of my clients over the years. They absolutely loved it!

How To Create a Remarkable Life

Imagine it's 10 years from now...

Envision the life you could have if you pursued everything you wanted with the certainty that you would succeed at every single thing you chose. In other words, you would have no failure or possibility of failure.

What does your life look like? What are you doing? Where are you living? Who are you living with? What kind of house are you in? Is it an apartment or a house? Do you live in the city or are you in the country? Do you have a significant other? Do you have children? Do you have pets? Do you have a car? What is your car like? What is your career like? What excites you? What is your health like?

Most of all, *are you happy?*

Give it a try; write down all of the details about your life ten years in the future. How would you describe your entire day from the moment you wake up to the moment you go to bed? Write it all down and do not edit. Put your whole heart into it. Write like your life depends on it. Don't share any of this with anyone other than yourself.

Review it regularly and see what happens.*

This exercise has a magical quality so you should be careful what you wish for!

Remember to dream big, without any fear.

Another way to Think Big is to start watching your language and 'pretending' to be the successful, happy and joyful person you want to be.

My dear friend Raymond and I used to play a game of creating the future by having a conversation with each other that congratulated us on our future achievements.

For example, I would say to Raymond (who hadn't written his book yet), *"I'm thrilled that your book is doing so well! I noticed it's number one on Amazon; wow, congratulations!!"* We decided to call it *The Remembering Game.*

Try it, it's fun.

This exercise came from Debbie Millman, a successful writer, artist, designer, and educator.

Chapter 4

Feel Good

To me, feeling good means having a happy and positive feeling about myself and my life, vibrant energy and a 'fun' attitude. Learning to feel good pretty much all of the time is not necessarily easy, depending on what's going on in your life. However, as we learnt through the previous chapters, your life is largely determined by your own personal choices and the decisions that you take in every area of your life. You've got to where you are now by the choices that you took, and if you want to change that, it's up to you to make new, different and better choices.

I don't remember exactly when I first heard the expression "Feel-Good Factor" but I do remember a book of that title by Patrick Holford published in 2010, and now that phrase has moved itself into our language.

Having just checked out on Google "feel-good factor," I realize that many people are using this expression for companies, businesses, books, courses, etc. In fact, feeling good has become quite an industry, so why do you think this happened? Possibly because people are not feeling good.

How are you feeling? Do you feel good, and what does feeling good mean to you?

I doubt if anybody wants to feel bad; it's a horrible feeling and nothing I would want to experience, so I'd rather put my energy into feeling good by doing things I know that bring me joy, keep me healthy, lift my spirits and raise my vibration.

Let's look at the different areas of our life. Here are a few questions for you to answer to see where you are on the Feel-Good Factor.

Are you happy with your job?

Are you happy with your home?

Do you like where you live?

Have you chosen wonderful friends that love and support you?

Do you experience good health?

Do you love yourself?

Do you exercise, eat well, laugh a lot?

How do you feel when you get up in the morning?

Do you feel you've had enough rest, are you ready to start your day, or would you rather stay in bed?

When you're feeling good on all levels, e.g., physically, emotionally, mentally, and spiritually, you're usually ready to jump out of bed and start your day because you know it's going to be wonderful. You know you're in charge of your day. You're not letting other people dictate to you what you should be doing, where you should be going, how to dress, or influence any other aspect of your life.

In fact, leave that word *should* out of our vocabulary as it's really irrelevant. You either do or you don't... no shoulds!

Let's look at the physical first.

Feeling good has a lot to do with how healthy you are.

Taking care of your body is vitally important. It's your vehicle, your avatar that travels with you on your journey through life, and much like having a car, it needs to be taken care of and tuned up regularly. You have to clean it, you have to give it good food and lots of water, it needs to be moved regularly and it also needs time to rest and recuperate, which is why sleep is so important. It's while we are sleeping that the body is repairing our cells, detoxifying toxins and generally keeping us working efficiently.

I first became aware of my physical health was when I was not feeling well. When I was younger, I often felt low, with no energy. My life as a child was pretty stressful and I was very unhappy a lot of the time. I suffered from migraines for years, I was mentally sluggish and just not feeling very good. I finally got sick of feeling like that and decided to do something about it. I started reading books on diet and health and exercise, and how to basically move into a feeling of good health.

It took a lot of discipline and quite a few changes to my diet and my mental perspective of life before I started seeing the new me. I joined a yoga class. I joined a gym. I became vegetarian and started being conscious about the food I ate. It was at this time that I started to get interested in healing and started taking classes on how to heal myself, so my own healing really was the first place I started.

I studied Reiki, Crystal Healing, Labyrinths, Aromatherapy, Cranial Sacral Therapy and Kinesiology. I also added Sound, Color and Light to my list of classes and qualifications. I have continued to study different ways of healing every year as the subject is infinite and there is always something amazing to learn which enables me to help others. As I write this, I am starting my training to become a Qigong practitioner!

I think a lot of healers actually are able to do the work that they do because they've experienced for themselves what it's like to be unhealthy, to be overweight, to be depressed. The first step is to make a decision... decide you want to feel better; you want to feel good, and then you can take the appropriate actions to make that happen.

No two people are alike. Every single person on this planet is bio-chemically individual so there is no definitive diet or exercise program that is ideal for everyone; you have to find it for yourself, often by trial and error. If you are a speedy person, for instance, with a fast job and high adrenaline, you may find that exercise like yoga calms you down; I know I did.

It was during my yoga classes that I learned about food and decided to become vegetarian. This is not for everyone and I'm not advocating that everyone should be vegetarian or even a vegan, however, it suited me at the time. I felt my digestion working so much better and realized that I was lighter both in mind and body. I also started meditating, which was perfect for me as I have a very busy brain and I often found it very hard to go to sleep.

To find your ideal diet you may decide to see a nutritionist and get some advice about what you can eat that suits you. There are so many 'diets' and 'fads' when it comes to food, so it's up to you to find the right diet for *you*.

As a Kinesiologist*[1], I am able to test what foods are beneficial for my clients and which foods are not. It's important to find the foods that *give* you energy rather than the ones that *take* it away from the body. It's also important to find out if you have any pathogens like parasites, bacteria, fungus, metal poisoning, radiation, etc. Once these are removed from the body, you will feel lighter, cleaner and have a much better level of health.

The next step is increasing your *'happiness energy'*.

This is the energy that makes you feel good by doing the little things that bring you joy. Surrounding yourself with people and things that bring you happiness.

Have you heard of oxytocin?

There's a hormone called oxytocin; it's been in the press quite a lot recently. This hormone is released by the pituitary gland and is often called the *'love drug'* because it is released when people get close and when you fall in love. It's that wonderful feeling of bliss. Having people around us who we love and who love us makes us feel wonderful. It's easy to feel lonely on your own for too long, but we can increase our level of oxytocin by doing a few simple things, so that we feel happier.

Your attention. Have you noticed how much time we all spend on our devices, be they phones, tablets or computers? We tend to be staring at machines and devices all the time, even when someone's talking to us. Have you noticed that often when you are having a conversation with someone, they keep checking their phone, or maybe you do? They are unable to give you their full attention.

To feel good about the connection with another person, it's important to give them your full attention. Connect with their eyes when you're talking or listening to them, learn to be present and you will both get more pleasure from your time together. It's amazing how much you miss when you are constantly looking at your phone.

Spoil yourself. I have to say I have leant how to spoil myself and I love it! Take good care of yourself. Do the things that give you great joy and pleasure on a regular basis, whatever that is for you. I like walking in the park, being in nature, taking a salt bath, spending time with friends. Telling people you love them and hearing it back creates a warm fuzzy feeling inside. Treat yourself once in a while to that special food, drink or outing that you put off for special occasions.

You are the most important person in your life, as I think we've said before, so treat yourself the way that you wish to be treated; don't wait for someone else to do it for you.

By doing things that make you happy you will start feeling good and that feeling will spread into other areas of your life, bringing health and happiness.

Giving. I learnt very early on that you can't really enjoy receiving unless you can give, and you can't really enjoy giving unless you can receive. So often this isn't the case. I know for myself that I found it very difficult to receive, but I loved giving and it took me quite a few years to get that balance right. Once I had, I got complete pleasure and joy from both giving and receiving.

The feeling of giving is a feeling of goodness. It gives pleasure not only to the giver but to the receiver. Giving can be just a smile! And receiving is just as important, as you are giving the giver the pleasure of giving!

Change Your Routine. Make a change in your daily routine, take a different route to work, or find one that suits you better and makes you... Feel Good. By changing your routine and taking life a little slower, you start to notice things in your life that you may not have noticed before. Sometimes we're moving so fast it's as though we forget to stop and smell the roses. It's those little tiny things that can make us feel good, like noticing the flowers and the seasons, hearing the birds singing outside your window in the morning, or a smile that stranger gave you as you pass them in the street. All these little things that change our feeling for the day and make us feel good.

Happy memories. I'm sure there have been times in your life where you were happy and took pictures to record those times and events. I have a huge box of photographs (memories) from years ago, before phones, and every now and then I'll sit down and go through them. I'm reminded of wonderful times with friends and family in beautiful situations like parties, holidays, Christmas, etc. By taking time to remember all those fabulous memories, it puts me in a place of joy and happiness. So, get out those old photo albums, or your phone, and look through all those wonderful pictures of times you were having fun with family and friends. Remind yourself what a fabulous life you had up to this point and that it can only get better.

Music. This is my favorite way to feel good. Music soothes the soul, raises the vibration and generally changes your mood.

As a Sound Healer, I was recently teaching a Tuning Forks Sound Class when I was asked what type of music I listen to. I mentioned the fact that when I'm doing the cleaning, I like to listen to something loud and fast like rock 'n' roll or dance music, however, at the end of the day I like to put on gentle classical music or something soothing like meditation or frequency music because I know that music changes your mood. By playing the right kind of music in the morning when you get up and are getting ready for work, you can start your day feeling really good. Then use music throughout the day to match the moods you desire.

Research shows that music is not only able to affect your mood – listening to particularly happy or sad music also changes your perception of your life.

I use different tones, frequencies and music for healing. Everything is vibration including us, so by using sounds, music and frequencies, we can bring ourselves back into balance.

Find a Way to Feel Good... no matter what it is!

Make feeling good important in everything you do.

Love is the highest vibration in the Universe, so by feeling love you will automatically be feeling good!

---

1. *Energy Medicine that address the physical, mental, chemical and energetic aspects of the body*
   https://www.kinesiologyassociation.org

Chapter 5

Take Responsibility

The most important aspect of your life is to acknowledge that it is your responsibility. No one can live your life for you. You are in charge.

This one is a biggie, and one that many people haven't really spent much time thinking about. It's time to take responsibility for your life, your actions, your situation... for *you*! Once you understand that you create your life, you are no longer just reacting to it, you are back in the driving seat!

Taking responsibility for yourself gives you true freedom.

Almost everything in our life, we have created with our thoughts, feelings, words and actions. We have covered this in the previous chapters, so I know you have a better understand of the power of your thoughts and words.

When things go wrong, we often like to blame others, but, in fact, that doesn't really work. Taking responsibility for yourself is empowering and will put you back in charge and take you from Victim to Victor!

We all have to grow up at some point, and as a grown-up, we are in charge of our life and we can no longer blame our parents, teachers, bosses, friends or anyone outside of ourselves for what happened in the past.

Whatever is going on in your life right now is your creation. In fact, your outside world, the life you have created, is a mirror of what's going on inside you. You have the choice to either change it or embrace it... it's up to you. You choose to make decisions about your life. Decisions that suit you. The exciting thing is that you have the power to create the changes you want by realizing that only *you* are responsible for your choices.

Tom Campbell, a brilliant physicist who has studied consciousness intently, has scientifically proven that we live in a virtual reality, which suggests that the purpose of our life here on earth is all about choice. We can make choices towards love or choices toward fear... that's all there is to it... it's that simple. Once we start taking responsibility for our choices we realize where perhaps we made ones along the way that were not for our highest good. In which case, it's time to change and make new ones. And remember, it's always possible to change your mind and make new choices that brings you joy.

You are in charge!

Complaining, blaming and generally taking everything personally will not bring you the life you desire... it will bring you more of the same, complaining, blaming and taking it personally.

Energetically, *"like attracts like,"* which means you attract energies that are harmonious with yours. If you think a certain way, you will often be attracted to others that think that way, that are on the same page, so to speak. Once you have decided what your beliefs and opinions are, based on your own intuition and research, you may find you meet others who think similarly to you.

So, it's a good idea to become the responsible person you want to be so that you attract people and situations that are in line with your desires and goals and thereby gain control over your life.

I left home very early, at 15, actually. My home life wasn't good and I couldn't wait to get out. It was then that I had to take responsibility for myself. I had to find work, find a place to live, etc. I found a flat to share in the evening paper and moved into a flat in London with four other girls who I had never met before. It was quite an adventure. We all had very little money so we shared everything we had for bills and food. We were all the same size so were able to share our clothes, too.

I had a day job as a trainee buyer in a department store, and an evening job in a pizza place so I got to eat. I learnt how to budget my money so that I had enough for the rent, etc., and enough left over for food and a little bit of fun!

I had attracted a lovely group of girls who were pretty much in the same situation as I was, so we all helped each other. A couple of them were a few years older than me and taught me how to take care of myself. This was my first experience of being completely on my own and being responsible for everything in my life. That experience taught me a lot and when I look back, I smile, because it was the best lesson ever, and helped me to take control of my life and learn independence which has held me in good stead all of my life.

In my work as a healer and teacher, I come across people constantly who are unwell, unhappy and are unsure why. Once we talk about their lifestyle, their emotional state, the food they eat, etc., and find ways to help change the areas that are not benefiting them, it's amazing how quickly they return to good health. They decide to take responsibility for their own health and well-being... as we all can. It's not always easy, but well worth it.

Have a look at the issues you have. Where did they come from? Do you have health issues, relationship issues, money issues? Are you happy with your life... where you live, where you work, who your friends are? If not, it may be time for you to have a very good look at your life and make some changes.

I had a good hard look at my life at one point, and once I decided to take responsibly for my life, I started making a conscious effort to change. It took time to address all these issues and find out where they came from. Using various therapies like the ones I have mentioned throughout this book I was able to clear the negative programming I had unconsciously taken on from parents, society, school, etc.

I used 'The Cleansing Prayer' (on the next page) which helped me...

The Cleansing Prayer

I am now choosing to cleanse myself and release any and all thoughtforms, beings, situations and energies that are no longer for my Highest and greater good, across all planes of my existence, across all Universes and across all lifetimes.

I ask that all energies that are less than LOVE be transmuted for the highest good of all... and so it is.

Decide if you want to make changes and then figure out how to do this. You may need some help from a professional therapist, healer or consultant. The most important thing is that you *want* to take your power back, which means taking responsibility for your life.

So, *"where to start?"*, you may say. Here are some suggestions to get you going and find that power within to become in control of your life.

1. Stop making excuses and eliminate blame... for everything. Whether that's to do with your health, finances, work or relationships, decide to take back your power and be in charge of your thoughts, words and actions.

How many times have you said or thought... *"If only I had more money, I'd..."*

Or, *"If I had more time, I'd..."*

You get what you focus on... so focus on the outcome you wish to create. See yourself happy and vibrant, full of energy achieving all the goals you have set yourself and being open to miraculous surprises. Appreciate what you *do* have and don't put energy into focusing on what you don't have.

This goes back to a previous chapter: Gratitude. You have created your life with so many things to be grateful for. Just embrace that and stop using excuses. This will relieve you of the 'wanting' and allow you to appreciate all the wonderful things you have. Using the emotion of 'wanting' is putting out to the Universe that you 'want'... so you will keep on 'wanting' as you always get what you ask for!

To consciously create your life with responsibility, *act,* don't *react.*

Don't allow other people to decide what's best for you; decide for yourself.

. . .

2. You are important.

I often ask clients to make a list of the five most important people in their lives. Invariably, they are not on the list!! That's a big eye opener. If you give all your energy away, and don't take care of yourself, it is you who will suffer. *You* are the most important person in your life. Take care of yourself first. When you are healthy and happy, you will have so much more energy for all the people in your life that you love and care about. Remember, every thought you have, every choice you make matters. It's creating your reality.

We become what we think about most

— Earl nightingale

3. Be kind.

When we take responsibility for ourselves, we don't allow others to treat us badly because we respect ourselves; we have boundaries, and we understand that we get back what we give out.

Choose to do things to make yourself feel good and that brighten someone's day, like smiling at people more often. You will find that when you are kind and you help others, it will come back to you, and when you are in need, others will help you too.

4. And have fun!!

I think we all take life far too seriously. We have this wonderful emotion called *humor* which is available to use 24/7 so why not use it a little more and see the fun side of life.

Laughter is the best medicine, so be sure to laugh a lot and share that wonderful energy with everyone you meet.

Remember, *you* are in charge of your life!!!

Chapter 6

Overcoming Challenges

They are part of life's rich pattern, those unexpected happenings that turn up out of nowhere and challenge you.

We all get them at some point in our lives. I know I've had many. It could be a physical or mental challenge, the breakdown of a marriage, problems with children, health issues, all kinds of challenges. Believe me, there's not going to be one person who doesn't have one, because actually it's through our challenges that we grow.

It's how we decide to handle these unexpected experiences, how we accept them that makes the difference. It's not always easy to handle the struggles that come from adversity. However, it's often in these times, that we find out who we really are, and learn that we have much more strength and courage than we thought.

Sometimes the lessons that we learn through difficult situations, even though they may be painful, make us stronger.

Obstacles in your way aren't meant to stop you, although it seems like that at the time. They are designed to point the way to new ways, new possibilities, and new opportunities.

Strength doesn't come from what you can do, but often from what you couldn't do. It makes you bigger, makes you stronger and more alive. If there were no challenges, your life would be pretty boring; everything would be the same every day. You'd know exactly where you're going, what you are going to do and how you are going to do it. There would be no surprises... and you wouldn't grow!

It's typical, isn't it, that challenges always seem to come at the most inopportune moments, when you least expect them and when you really don't want them. No matter what area of your life they are related to, they upset your daily routine, and the way your life is currently working. It's called *throwing a spanner in the works*!!

I can give you a really good example of that with something that happened to me. I was going about my life perfectly happy and healthy when lo and behold I tripped on a large piece of concrete in the street outside my home and landed flat on the ground. I'd managed somehow to slide along the gravel and cut up the left side of my face; my right arm had come up to save me (thank goodness), and I ended up with torn ligaments and tendon in my arm, my shoulder out of place, my back out of whack and a sprained wrist and thumb.

I consider myself very lucky now when I look back as I could've easily broken a bone, my nose, or lost a tooth. My first reaction was shock, and then I checked my teeth and my nose... a big sigh of relief and gratitude came over me when I realized they were intact. Mind you, I was very shaken and upset and spent quite a few weeks healing.

During this healing process, I learnt some new skills!

Being right-handed, it was very unfortunate that it was my right arm that was damaged, so I had to learn to use my left arm and hand. This was not easy. The first thing I noticed was how difficult it was to clean my teeth with my left hand, to turn the key in my car, cut up vegetables, or to open the door knob. I could've easily got very angry at myself for falling over or blamed the gravel on the ground for tripping me but actually I started to think how funny it was that I was forced to use my left arm, and my left hand.

I kept thinking, *"I'm becoming ambidextrous – how cool is that?"*

This accident slowed me down quite a bit, which isn't a bad thing as I'm pretty speedy.

I was looking for the positives and one of them was the amazing support I had from my friends and how wonderful my doctor was. I am lucky enough to have a few very special friends in my life and this made me appreciate them even more. It also pushed me to ask for help which is something I have always found difficult, being so independent.

My accident also had some good points; it's not been all bad, although I have to say I got rather tired of not being able to use my right wrist. With my knowledge of healing, I was able to facilitate a speedy recovery with my shoulder and arm and waited patiently (not something I'm good at, patience) for the full use of my right wrist, which took a few months.

It was my attitude to the challenge that made it bearable.

Other challenges may involve work. This could be public speaking or taking a new position in a company, or even a change in career.

When you're given an opportunity to do something you've never done before, it throws you out of your comfort zone. You can become nervous and insecure which makes you question your ability, but by pushing through and accepting the challenge, the prize is growth.

I think the most difficult challenges we face in life are heartache and loss. Whether it's the death of a family member or friend, a broken relationship or marriage, we feel devastated when this happens. It's as though life just stops, and we feel we are outside looking in with pain in our hearts and souls. It's at times like this that the support of friends and family is so invaluable.

Allow yourself the space to grieve the loss, don't try to be stoic and strong. It's *appropriate* to release the sadness of these times by crying and letting go of the pain. Eventually, believe me, it will pass, and you may start remembering all the wonderful memories and happy times you had.

I find it helpful to put up happy photos of people who have departed so that I am easily reminded of how lucky I was to have had them in my life, and how much I still love them.

So, how are we to handle all these challenges? Here are some suggestions...

- *Trust* that you are capable of handling any situation that comes into your life. If you are still here, you have managed to do that at some point.
- *Be still,* calm your mind by meditating or contemplating on the situation, and then let it go. Often, it's when we let go that the solutions appear.
- *Look for the positives.* I realized how lucky I was that my injury wasn't worse. Having a positive attitude is a big PLUS!
- *Give yourself a break* and take some time out. By giving yourself some space, you can start seeing your situation with much greater clarity. Sometimes all it takes is just going for a walk to clear your mind. Once your mind is clear, you will start to see your situation in a positive light, and you may even find ways to

deal with it that you hadn't thought of
before.

One of the biggest challenges for me, and for many of us, is the belief that we need to be independent and strong all the time... and we don't!

Believe me, changing our way of thinking is not something that comes easily at first. However, once you allow yourself to accept that you have the courage to ask for help, you may be pleasantly surprised at how kind people are and how much they enjoy helping you when you really need it.

I know it really helped me.

Here's a recap on some ways to overcome your challenges:

- See the gift in every situation
- Clear your mind... give yourself some space, take a walk
- Don't blame yourself
- Keep going... don't give up
- Create the outcome you desire by focusing on it
- Stay calm... meditate

- Change your perspective
- Ask for help
- Surround yourself with positive people
- Overcome your fears by facing them
- Practice patience.

These are things I have found to be helpful when facing obstacles and challenges.

I find they come up every now and then to move me into the next phase of my life, or to bring out qualities that haven't been exposed before. I found writing this book extremely challenging; it's something I've never done before and wasn't sure it would be of benefit to anyone... or that anyone would be interested. I managed to overcome that 'fear' with the help of my supportive friends and my writing coach.

I finally asked for help... it made all the difference!

Chapter 7

Watch Your Words

If you want to find the secrets of the universe, think in terms of energy, frequency and vibration. – Nikola Tesla

I t may sound odd, but did you know that talking to your cells improves your health?

It has been proven that each cell is a thinking cell, an intelligent cell, so it makes perfect sense to communicate with them. After all, they are you!! They are what makes up you!!

So, *why not get to know yourself at a cellular level?*

When studying Cranial Sacral Therapy, I was introduced to John Upledger's book, *Cell Talk*. That book, together with learning Cranial Sacral Therapy and Kinesiology, introduced me to a new way of 'talking' to the body, which I have incorporated in my healing work ever since.

At the quantum level, we are all just big bundles of energy.

So, *what is energy?*

The entire Universe is made up of vibrations, and everything within the Universe is Vibrational Energy... including yourself. Therefore, Vibration = Energy. *Everything* is energy.

Our thoughts are energy, our words, our emotions are energy, even the chair you are sitting on is vibrating with energy.

You can actually alter your own vibration by changing the way you think, feel, or act. You see, whatever you choose to think has consequences, and therefore whatever you say also has consequences. You are designing your own life with your thoughts and then bringing them into fruition with your words. Pretty cool, hey?

Each word has a frequency, and that can either be a positive energy frequency or a negative one. Ideally, you want to reside in a positive frequency so that your life is easy and flowing without struggle. The thing to remember is that you have a relationship with your body.

Your body is listening to you... all the time! You are in charge.

If you keep stating and telling your body you are unhappy, overweight, depressed, etc., it will continue to give you those situations. You are the boss of your body, and you are saying to your body *"I am miserable"* so the message goes through to all the cells... "Hey guys, we are miserable... ok, got it!!"... and they will respond by giving you what you stated.

Now, if you tell your body, *"I am happy"* (even if you are not), by stating that enough times the message goes to all the cells. *"I am happy"* becomes the new message, and slowly the *"I am miserable"* dissipates... making you feel a lot happier. It may take a few days or even weeks of making positive statements depending on where you are at, but believe me, it works.

Think of the time you were at school and you were learning your times table – you repeated them over and over until you knew it perfectly... it became an inherent knowing. The same applies to all the words you use.

Your cells believe everything you say.

It is almost impossible for your body to change when you keep giving it negative messages like, "I'm ugly, old, miserable, unhappy, etc.," so, change your words and change your life!!

Some people have a hard time saying positive statements when that is not their current reality, as it doesn't feel real and I totally understand, because it isn't... *yet*!

The point is, if you want to change your reality, you have to start changing the way you think and speak. Changing the negative "I am" to a positive "I am" is a great place to start and works at a cellular level.

Your body's intelligence, the innate intelligence, is extremely smart. The body is always striving towards a healthy mind and body, yet the power of your mind has the ability to disrupt this natural outcome, especially when you are constantly feeding it negativity.

Love yourself in your current condition, stop abusing your body with thoughts and words. Once you start loving your body (and yourself in general), you will be amazed at how it will start working even harder for you to get the results your desire.

I started using affirmations many years ago when I was consciously looking to change my life.

The first book I got that introduced me to affirmations and how they affect the body was Louise Hay's book *You Can Heal Your Life*. I still have my copy from 1984! It was a godsend at the time, and since then I have recommended it to hundreds of people. It is still in print today and has sold over 50 million copies... so it must work!!!

I decided to use affirmations as medicine about 20 years ago when I really understood the importance of talking to your cells, and the frequency of words. That information has helped me and many hundreds of my clients to shift their perception, change their attitude and heal their body.

The following are just some of my favorite affirmations that I use myself and give to my clients:

I am happy, healthy and fit.
I love myself unconditionally.
I enjoy each day.
My life is full of wonderful surprises.
I have never felt better.
I am financially stable and free from debt.
I am the healthiest I have ever been.

I'm sure you can find others that suit you perfectly. Start by saying them 10 times with your eyes open (in the conscious world) and 10 times with your eyes closed (the subconscious).

Start with just a few and say them daily. Then watch how your perception of life starts to shift and life becomes easier.

You can change the affirmations to suit your situation, as that will change constantly.

The main thing to remember is that *you* control your thoughts. No one tells you what to think... *you* decide, and realizing that, *you* decide your future!

Chapter 8

Practice Forgiveness

The forgiving state of mind is a magnetic power for attracting good.

— Catherine Ponder

It is easier to forgive an enemy than to forgive a friend.

— William Blake

F orgiveness needs a section to itself as it's so important on your journey to waking up and higher consciousness. It is amazingly effective in clearing old emotions and hurts and releasing yourself from the pain of the past.

Forgiveness is a powerful word... to some, a scary word. According to Wikipedia, "It's the process of ceasing to feel resentment, indignation, or anger against another person for a perceived offense, difference or mistake, or ceasing to demand punishment or restitution."

I feel that forgiveness is a healing journey. I found it to be a very necessary part of my healing process that released me from the anger and hurt that I carried.

Even if you know in your heart that you want or need to forgive someone, the path to achieving it can be quite difficult. However, I found that once achieved it brings with it its own kind of peace. Peace that is deep and fulfilling... a feeling of release from the pain and anger you have unwittingly been holding on to.

It takes courage to forgive, not only others but most of all yourself.

We are so hard on ourselves. We are constantly beating ourselves up for not being good enough, for not achieving, for reasons too numerous to mention.

When someone you care about hurts you, you make a decision. You can hold on to the anger, resentment and thoughts of revenge, or embrace forgiveness and move forward. And that is where the feelings of joy and happiness lie, in those moments when you decide to let go of the pain.

This doesn't mean you have to forget what happened, but forgiveness can lessen its grip and help you focus on other positive parts of life. Forgiveness also doesn't mean that you deny the other person's responsibility for hurting you, and it doesn't minimize or justify the wrong.

You can forgive the person without excusing the act.

From my experience, you just come to a better place of understanding and realize how detrimental it is to *you* to not forgive them. Often you find that whatever the issue is, the person who wronged you has forgotten all about it and it is *you* who is holding on to the hurt and anger, not them. You are the one who is suffering. You are the one living in the past and dragging that pain around with you, dumping it into every relationship and situation you find yourself in *now*.

So, let's do something about that.

Forgiveness applies to all of us. Nearly everyone has been hurt by the actions or words of another. But when you don't practice forgiveness, you may be the one who pays most dearly. By embracing forgiveness, you embrace peace, hope, gratitude and joy.

From the spiritual point of view, forgiveness is living from the heart, releasing the past situations and people who may have hurt or abused you, and realizing that every day gives you the opportunity to be free from the pain of not forgiving, be it yourself or someone else.

Here is an example from my life...

As a child, I didn't know who my mother was. She died when I was very young and no-one ever mentioned her. When I asked my dad about her, who she was, what happened to her, he just ignored me. This went on throughout my life, and it wasn't until I was 27 that an aunt decided I deserved to know and told me about her, and I then found out that I was the survivor of twins... *I was a twin!*

I asked my dad yet again if he could talk to me about my mother, and again he just ignored me.

I realized before he passed that I needed to forgive him. Rather than be angry with him, which I had been, I forgave him as I didn't really know why he was unable to talk to me about her. Whatever the reason, it was *his* reason and not for me to judge. I forgave him and in return felt a bond with him that I had never had, plus I felt 'lighter' having dumped the anger and resentment I held towards him.

What are the benefits of forgiving someone?

Researchers have recently become interested in studying the effects of forgiveness. Evidence is mounting that holding on to grudges and bitterness results in long-term health problems. Forgiveness offers numerous benefits, including:

- Lower blood pressure
- Stress reduction
- Less hostility
- Better anger management skills
- Lower heart rate
- Lower risk of alcohol or substance abuse
- Fewer depression symptoms
- Fewer anxiety symptoms
- Reduction in chronic pain
- More friendships
- Healthier relationships
- Greater religious or spiritual well-being
- Improved psychological well-being.

Forgiveness is a commitment to a process of change, and as we know change can be difficult and can take time. We all move toward forgiveness a little differently.

The first step is to recognize the value of forgiveness and its importance in our lives. Another is to reflect on the facts of the situation, how we've reacted to it, and how this combination has affected our lives, our health and our well-being. Then, when we are ready, we can actively choose to forgive the one who has offended us. In this way, we move away from our role as a victim and release the control and power the offending person and situation has had in our lives.

Forgiveness also means that we change old patterns of beliefs and actions that are driven by our bitterness (which shows up in the gallbladder). As we let go of grudges, we no longer define our lives by how we've been hurt, and we may even find compassion and understanding.

Forgiveness takes away the power the other person continues to hold over you. Through forgiveness, you choose to no longer define yourself as a victim. Forgiveness is done primarily for yourself, less so for the person who wronged you.

Here's an idea that worked for me when I needed to address forgiveness.

I had to accept the fact that like everyone else, I'm not perfect. I had to *accept* myself despite my faults and admit my mistakes. I had to be completely honest with myself and commit to treating others with compassion, empathy and respect.

What to do:

1. Write a letter to yourself, forgiving yourself for anything you feel is required. No one else will ever see this letter, so don't hold back. Say it all... everything. Imagine you are outside of yourself; how would you forgive *you?*

2. Now, make a list of people in your life you want to forgive.

3. Write a letter of forgiveness to all of them. Writing with honesty and compassion. Understanding that they did what they did with the information they had at the time. They are not you and do not think as you do. They are coming from a different place.

4. Don't send these letters. Burn them once you have written them and send them out into the ethers, with the intention of lovingly releasing them. The actual act of writing the letters releases *you,* and on an energetic level the other person or situation.

By now, you know that I like to use affirmations to clear old thoughts and feelings.

Words have the power to release and change your perception by overriding the existing thoughtforms and replacing them with new more positive ones.

I found this affirmation to be particularly helpful:

"*I am able to forgive.*" Say it with feeling, maybe looking in the mirror? You need to believe you are able to forgive, for the process to work.

Here are some other suggestions:

- I forgive all people who have wronged me both real and perceived
- I surround myself with people who I love and respect and who love and respect me
- I forgive myself
- I forgive others
- I release all anger which allows me to forgive
- I release all guilt which allows me to forgive
- It is safe for me to forgive
- I am open to receive forgiveness.

How did that feel?

You may need to say them daily for a couple of weeks to start feeling the benefit. I suggest saying them with your eyes closed, accessing the subconscious as that is where a lot of unexpressed emotions reside.

Feel free to change them to words that you feel are beneficial to you... remember *you* are in charge!

> *When you hold resentment toward another, you are bound to that person or condition by an emotional link that is stronger than steel. Forgiveness is the only way to dissolve that link and get free.* – Catherine Ponder

Chapter 9

Get A Grip

Hey guys, it's time to grow up and... get a grip!

That sounds ominous doesn't it... growing up?? *What does that mean?*

From my perspective, it really just means taking responsibility for your life, for your choices and actions, no matter what they have been or are now.

It means no more winging, whining or moaning about why or how you can't have, be or do what you want to do in your life. No more blame (we've covered that in a previous chapter), and no more excuses.

What is it you want?

How do you wish your life to be? What is really important to you? What do you actually believe? Do you know?

It's time to take a good hard look at all these questions and many more... are you ready?

Before we begin, take a couple of deep breaths and find your center, that place inside you that is calm and at peace. *The true you.*

Breathe... There... that's better...

Firstly, we need to understand that our beliefs shape our thoughts and emotions. (We covered this in a previous chapter, Watch Your Words). This understanding is shown to us as our actions and behaviors, making what we tell ourselves and what we believe extremely important. We need to truly believe what we are saying to ourselves. We can tell ourselves that we're capable, successful, healthy or content... but do we really believe it or are they just words with no intention behind them?

> *Intention is not something you do, but something you connect to. When you change the way you look at things, the things you look at change. A truly scientific fact.*
>
> — *Dr. Wayne Dyer*

The power of intention is the most powerful force in the Universe.

You must have a strong desire and intention to create what you want. There is no room for wishy-washy thinking... thought into action is what is required.

Intention is the underlining power to bring to fruition your goals and dreams, no matter how big or small. Intention is more important than the way you wish to create a situation, goal or desire. It creates an energy behind all those desires to allow them to materialize in the best way for your highest good; however, you need to be really clear and honest with yourself about what you want to create.

For example, my intention is to help as many people as possible with my healing skills and talents, so I start my day asking, *"How can I be of service?"* I know that is my underlying intention... not a specific way of achieving it but allowing it to show itself.

Most of our beliefs and actions have been with us for many years, maybe even from childhood, and I understand how difficult it is to break away from old habits – it took me a while. Habits of blaming the government, your parents, the weather... basically anything, or anyone besides yourself when things don't go the way you would like them to. That has to stop!

You may not have ever really experienced your true potential, and the power of authenticity. Changing these 'old' habits is a good start to becoming the true you.

I know it's not easy to take charge of *everything* in your life, but as you do, little by little, you will start to be empowered with the understanding that you are in control of your life, and that's an amazing feeling.

Let's look at the questions above.

What is it you want and how do you want your life to be?

Do you know? Have you taken the time to look deep into yourself to find the truth of what you want.?

Most people automatically say they want money, health, a new car, a relationship, a great job, their own business, etc., etc., and some of you may have already gotten those things.

However, I think what we tend to forget is that often those things come and go. They give us pleasure for a period of time, but often not forever.

Why not create things for yourself that are lasting, like joy, peace, love, health and abundance?

Once we have achieved those qualities in ourselves, you'll be amazed at how they affect your decision-making process, so that you start making decisions that are in alignment with your best discernment.

We all have to face what is going on in the world, and as I write this chapter in 2020, it's a mess. However, it's not about what is happening out there, but how we handle it that makes the difference in our own personal experience of our physical reality. And after all, life is just an experience that we are having, and once we understand that, we can get a grip and take control. We can then change our experience to a different one, one that serves us better. It's all down to how we react to circumstances.

It's down to our perspective!

Our physical reality is basically a reflection of what's going on in our belief systems: the outcome of our actions and choices. Physical reality is nothing more than a mirror based on the beliefs we hold to be true. The ones we have accumulated throughout our lives.

What do you believe? Do you believe you have choice? Do you believe you are good enough? Do you believe you are loveable?

The answers to all these questions and many more contribute to the world (reality) you have created for yourself.

Take time to answer these questions. Be honest and think about them. Take the opportunity to change some of your beliefs to create more of what you want in your life. You can't change your life unless you are prepared to do 'the work.' Discipline and focus are what's needed, and *now* is a good time to put them into practice.

Although we may have experienced some negative experiences in our lives, and most of us have, if we can learn the lessons from them, we can then extract a beneficial and positive outcome. It's time to let go of the fear-based beliefs that created the experience in the first place and start going in a positive direction. Look at one of your negative experiences and say to yourself, "What did I learn from this?"

As a healer working with many people, I find that we all have negative issues we wish to release, and my job is to help clear those emotions so that you can move forward with a healthy mind, body and soul, and create a new version of yourself.

I can give you the tools and techniques, but *you* have to do the work.

I am just the facilitator to help you to become the next *best* version of yourself!

Go ahead, get started... there is now time like the present!

Chapter 10

Be Kind

Kindness is one of the most beautiful qualities we have. It is defined as being friendly, generous, compassionate and considerate... it's a virtue... and it costs nothing.

We all have this wonderful quality within us; whether we use it or not is another story. If we're not using it, or aware of it, maybe life has got so difficult that we've just forgotten, or it's been too long since we even considered it or experienced it.

I believe that kindness is inherent in us all.

Can you remember a time when you experienced giving an act of kindness? Did you help a stranger, give someone a compliment or even just hold the door open for someone?

A smile, a compliment, listening, helping someone with directions, these are all acts of kindness that can make a huge difference not just to the person who received the 'act' but to you, too.

When you offered an act of kindness, what did it feel like? Did you get a feeling of satisfaction, did it open your heart and make you feel good? That's the feeling you give/get when you act out of kindness.

Often, it's the small acts of kindness to others that have the ability to change someone's day for the better.

Can you remember the last time someone was kind to you? Was it a parent, a lover, a sibling, a friend or maybe even a stranger? Was it a birthday gift, a bunch of flowers or a compliment?

Stop for a moment and try to remember the feeling of kindness given to you.

How did it feel? Did it make you feel happy, worthy, grateful, or warm and fuzzy? Did it change the way you were feeling at the time?

There are so many ways you can show kindness. For instance, once I was in a supermarket, and the man behind me was obviously homeless. He wanted to buy a couple of bottles of beer and some chips. After I had completed my purchase, I asked the assistant to charge me for his items. She was quite shocked and said, "You want to pay for his beer?" I just nodded and said yes. I wanted to help him, by not making a fuss, just by paying for his chosen items, as he was struggling with change to make sure he had enough. He said, "Thank you," I smiled and said, "You're welcome," and that was that.

When I left the supermarket, I felt good. Not an 'ego' good but a heartfelt good. I got pleasure from helping someone, and I realized that I could be doing more of that.

A lesson in kindness I have experienced is from my granddaughter Zoe who always asks me if she can give change to any homeless person she sees. Naturally, I say yes, and she gets great pleasure giving them money. She smiles at them and tells them to have a nice day... in fact, she tells everyone she interacts with to have a nice day... always with a big smile. She is one of the kindest people I know.

Times when we forget kindness are when our emotions get the best of us. Staying calm at all times, and not getting mad, cross or angry with others is a wonderful idea and sounds very easy.

I am reminded of when I took my first Reiki class many years ago. I was taught the principles of Reiki, which is a hands-on healing technique using Universal Life Energy. According to Dr. Usui who brought Reiki to the world, by living your life according to Reiki Principles you will live a happy and fulfilled life. One of those principles was, "Just for today, do not anger."

Sounds easy enough, I thought... ha-ha... I soon found out I was wrong. It wasn't as easy as I thought it would be to let go of anger... well it wasn't at first. It took time.

The thing is, I actually didn't feel I had any anger inside me; I thought I was just fine. In fact, it took me quite a few months of introspection and meditation to get to grips with the real meaning of that principle and to then incorporate it into my life.

I realized that releasing anger helps you to become kind, and kindness bring you nearer to peace.

It's amazing to find out how much we hold inside from past experiences and relationships.

I did 'the work' on myself, which included finding someone to help me. I was lucky enough to have studied Reiki (which I could do for myself) and know fellow therapists to call on. I used EFT[1] and Kinesiology to remove old programs and find the cause of any hidden subconscious negative emotions that I was holding on to. I connected with parts of myself that were still angry at certain people or situations, let them go, and things began to change. It wasn't easy, and meditation was a great help in finding my 'center' and calming my mind and body.

Being still and going 'inside' brings its own healing gifts.

Once I had a deep understanding of how detrimental unexpressed emotions are to the physical and emotional body and found ways to handle them, it was easier to let go and realize that often these feelings come from a place deep inside the subconscious and suppress our feelings of kindness.

When we find situations or people that trigger us, what's happening is it's the 'subconscious behavioral reaction' that comes from the 'back' brain or the amygdala. That is the part of the brain that acts automatically from memories of past behavior.

By changing our automatic reactions, consciously, to ones of kindness, we can then change our behavioral response to one of compassion.

As you know by now, I use affirmations as they work like vibrational medicine; they are positive and powerful statements or words that inspire and motivate us. Every cell in our body has innate intelligence and hears everything we think and speak. By telling your body good, strong, positive words, and repeating the affirmations, you start moving your mind in a new and more desirable direction. The benefits are a more positive perspective.

Many times, if not always, with a first-time client, I find that old issues are causing them distress to both the body and the mind and smothering the quality of kindness, especially the ability to be kind to themselves. There is a plethora of reasons for this, depending on each individual. By using my healing skills, I am able to offer suggestions using certain affirmations that test beneficial for them.

Here are just a few examples:

1. I choose to perform acts of kindness every day

2. I allow my subconscious to relax and feel peace

3. I'm spreading love and kindness all around me

4. I stay in my personal power at all times.

There are many more to choose from.

Kindness goes hand in hand with peace, and when you are at peace with yourself, kindness becomes automatic.

Kind words can work miracles, they can help heal wounded relationships, bring a smile to someone's face, make someone happy or clear feelings of sadness. Kindness is sweet, loving and considerate.

Not only do our acts of kindness help others but they make us feel good, too.

Remember to be especially kind to yourself. Love yourself, don't beat yourself up because you think you haven't achieved enough, or you don't look the part, or you don't have enough of this, that or the other. You are a unique being of love and light here on this planet for the experience of being *you*. How amazing is that?!!

Take time to really get to know yourself.

What do you like to do? How do you like to spend your free time? Accept yourself as you are; you can always change, that goes without saying, because change is constant. We all change all the time. However, it's important to love yourself in every moment and be kind to yourself always.

Kindness promotes empathy and compassion, and by being kind and gentle to yourself you will find it so much easier to be kind to others.

Kindness can lift up anyone's spirits and, believe it or not, you hold the power to make someone's day.

Start today with a small gesture of kindness, and make someone's day better. No matter how small or big the act of kindness may be, it makes a *huge* difference in you and in the person or people who received your act of kindness

It's important to clear any pent-up negative feelings you have if you want to find your kindness. You'll be surprised how much better you will feel once you have removed unresolved feelings and are clear.

Just think how different this world would be if everyone took a few minutes out of their week to do something for someone else.

So, let's make sure that random acts of kindness are happening every day in our lives... for no other reason other than it good to be kind.

---

1. Emotional Freedom Technique

Chapter 11

Laugh A Lot!!

We have now come to the final chapter in our handbook to *The Fast Track to Waking Up*, and it's one of my favorites.

Laughter is a wonderful, easy, pleasant and enjoyable way to lift our frequency so that we vibrate at a much higher state of awareness. It raises our consciousness, wakes us up and creates a better reality – which is the goal!

Enjoy life to the fullest by seeing the fun in it.

There's nothing better than a good laugh with friends and family, or even strangers, and the plus side is that it's fun and has a positive effect on your health. You have probably heard the expression, "Laughter is the best medicine."

Well, it's true!

Laughter releases tension, fear, and anxiety and lifts our spirits, fills us with joy and makes us feel better. It's also excellent at reducing stress levels. It actually lowers hormones like cortisol, adrenaline, dopamine and growth hormone and increases the level of health-enhancing hormones, and boosts our immune system... and we all need that... right?

Life is guaranteed to give us challenges, and as we've learnt, those challenges can help us grow if we have the right perspective, so it helps if we try not to take life too seriously. After all, life is meant to be fun, so why on earth would we have been given this wonderful quality of humor if we weren't meant to use it?

Can you remember a time when you were laughing your head off about something, or found the humor in a particular situation? Do you remember how that felt? For example, I have been known to spend time looking for my glasses only to realize they are on my head!

Was there a time when you cheered someone up by making them laugh? That felt good, didn't it?

Laughter is infectious, and the more we laugh, the higher we raise our vibration by filling our whole being with joy.

There has been many a time when I have heard someone else laughing and ended up joining in, having no idea at all what I was laughing at... I was just laughing... full-on belly laughing. The more I realized I had no idea what I was laughing at, the funnier it became.

I remember it happened once in a restaurant. I was with friends and someone on the table next to ours was howling with laughter, and by osmosis, I caught it. I started laughing so hard that I had to leave the table and go to the bathroom to contain myself. I stayed in there for a few minutes trying to stop and calm down. However, it took a while and when I finally thought I had it under control I left the bathroom and started walking towards our table. Before I actually got to the table, it hit me again so hard that I had to go back into the bathroom to settle down and compose myself yet again. This happened about three times before I was all laughed out, and able to return to the table in a fairly normal state.

It felt pretty amazing to be filled with uncontrollable laughter!

So far, I have managed to find the humor in life most of the time.

One of the things that keeps laughter away from our lives is getting stuck in negative thinking. These are the thoughts we have that are often subconscious. When we are expecting the worse, worrying about the future, or planning for something that may never happen, we are bathed in negative thinking, and that's when we start seeing the glass half empty.

Laughter often helps you to see a different, more positive outlook to the one you had at any one time and will also help you to find solutions to difficult situations. It's up to you to shift your 'old' pattern of negativity to one that is more positive where possible. It's not surprising that you may find this difficult, you are not alone.

Research has shown that people tend to focus more on the negative as they try to make sense of the world. It's the 'bad things' that happen, just look at the news for instance, that seem to grab our attention more easily than 'positive things' and, in many cases, this can influence our decisions.

I know it's not easy, but if you start with a little problem, and shift your perspective, you will be surprised how that translates to other larger situations in your life.

Children laugh all the time... and so can you!

I have a recording of people laughing that I acquired many years ago (it was on a cassette). All kinds of laughter from babies gurgling, to grown men howling with laughter and everything in between. I used to play it for my students and clients when it was appropriate. They were often quite bemused when I burst into laughter for no apparent reason, but soon found themselves laughing along with me as laughter is so infectious.

It's hard to be miserable when you are laughing!!

"Always Look on the Bright Side of Life" by Monty Python was a favorite of mine for cheering people up. And I'm sure you'll agree, we *all* need cheering up at times.

Life is not always easy, and I truly know how difficult and scary it can be – I've been there.

There were many times in my life that I would have been quite happy to throw in the towel. However, by some miraculous reason, I was blessed with friends who helped me laugh... about how nuts the world was, or how crazy some people were. How it wasn't worth taking it all so seriously.

Taking life too seriously has its costs. Health being one of them.

Depression is an epidemic these days with the uncertainty of where life is going and how we survive. When we are suffering from mental exhaustion, a good dose of laughter can help you feel good. The funny thing is that the feeling you get from a good laugh stays with you even once the laughter has subsided because you have changed your frequency. You are now on a lighter, brighter one.

Don't take yourself too seriously, either. We can all learn to love ourselves and laugh at the idiosyncrasies or muddles that we have.

Being dyslexic, I am known for constantly not being able to find the right word, or even pronounce it correctly! I often just laugh at myself when I get a word wrong, rather than feel embarrassed or beat myself up.

Obviously, there are things in life that need to be taken seriously, but there's nothing positive or healthy about taking your life so seriously that you end up turning every molehill into a mountain.

I believe that having the ability to laugh at ourselves is the secret to fully enjoying our lives.

Here are a few more ways to lift your spirits... and laugh!

They may seem pretty basic, but I know when you are feeling down, the idea of doing any of them can be overwhelming. So, just start with a few.

1. **Music**... music always affects your mood, so find pieces of music that make you feel good, something you love, and play it in the background while you get ready for your day. If it makes you feel like dancing... dance your socks off!

2. **Exercise**... now, hear me out, nothing too taxing, but something easy and enjoyable. You were introduced to Cross Crawl exercise in Chapter 1, but I feel it deserves another look!

Cross Crawl is perfect for integrating your right and left brain, which gives you more energy and looks kind of funny. So, it may make you laugh! It helps you to feel more balanced, think more clearly, improve your co-ordination and harmonize your energies.

And it's so easy...

- Touch one elbow or hand to the opposite knee. Touching the right elbow to the left knee and then the left elbow to the right knee, large areas of both brain hemispheres are activated at the same time.
- Do this for a few minutes. I like to do it for the length of a song or piece of music, and often it

will bring a big smile to my face as my body connects and harmonizes.

3. **Smile!** At your family members and people you pass in the street, or at the checkout person in the store. If you live alone, smile at your image in the mirror... smile and laugh with yourself! If this seems a bit odd, make a funny face to your mirror image that will make you laugh.

If you find it difficult to "force" a laugh, (like I did with my laughing tape) you have plenty of help on YouTube. There are masses of videos of babies laughing, which is really infectious, or funny animal videos to make you laugh ... that should do it!

Once you are free from the negative restraints that you have been captured by, life will soon seem light again. Fun will creep into your day, and having fun will bring you laughter you had forgotten was there

I think one of the attributes to being 'awake' and having awareness is that you can see the funny side of life. Knowing that this is just a journey, an experience, and knowing you can change yourself and your life by changing your thoughts, gives you the benefit of knowing that sometimes you just have to have a good hearty laugh at life!

Laughter is the key to *freedom*!!

Afterword

Raise Your Vibration

Now that you have read the book and are familiar with the 11 ways I have shared with you to Waking Up, you will see that by doing all of these suggestions the goal has always been to raise your vibration.

"What does 'raise your vibration' mean?" you may ask.

Let me explain...

Everything in the Universe is energy, and all energy vibrates as a unique frequency which creates sound. Whether we can hear it or not, vibrations are sound waves. Every thought creates vibrations. How often have you walked into a room and felt uncomfortable? You kind of know this is not your crowd, the feeling was not right for you, you didn't like the 'vibe.' That's because it didn't match your frequency. Then another time you walk into a room and feel really comfortable, this crowd is on your wave length, so to speak... they were resonating at a similar frequency to you. They had good vibes. That vibration felt good for you.

The question is... *why do you want to raise your vibration?*

I talk a lot about that.

Well, I'll tell you: it's simple.

The reason I wrote this little book and made it easy and simple to use is because when we use these principles, it makes us feel good and gives us the opportunity to live in harmony with ourselves and the planet.

We are all magnetic beings and as such we vibrate at a certain frequency. This frequency draws towards us people, places and things that resonate to our vibration. If you change your vibration, you change your frequency and will then, as magnetic beings, draw towards you people, places and situations that resonate to your new vibration.

If you want to experience love, joy, happiness, inspiration, abundance and great health – and let's face it, who doesn't? – then you have to vibrate at a higher vibration because those qualities vibrate higher than the negative ones.

Once you raise your vibration, you begin to change your perspective and see the bigger picture. You understand the importance of being *you* and begin to love yourself completely. You understand that giving and receiving are as important as each other. You begin to take notice of what you put in your body, and drink more water. You realize that what you put into life is what you get out, so you start to be aware of your thoughts and actions... it's a wonderful process.

Our body, organs, muscles, bones, etc., all vibrate at a certain frequency. When we are unwell, we are not vibrating at our optimum frequency for good health... we have dropped our frequency, and it is now discordant to us... we are in a state of ill health or dis-ease. So, we want to raise our vibration to get back to good health.

Every thought creates vibrations too, which is why it is *so important* to take care of your thoughts. We covered this in Chapter 7, Watch Your Words. No one makes you think something. It is your choice; your thoughts are *your* thoughts. If they are negative or self-destructive then they are resonating at a low vibration, and you will experience your life accordingly with maybe depression or illness.

If your thoughts are high vibration thoughts, positive thoughts, you will experience a positive outlook on life and draw towards you *good* energy... good vibes. This will make you feel good, healthier, be more aware of your body, take better care of yourself and generally enjoy life more. That's what I want for us all.

Simple, isn't it!?

Vibrational healing or energy healing has now become part of our everyday lives. There are numerous modalities that use it around the world, and many books have been written on the subject. I use it in my practice and teach it as Reiki, Sound Therapy and Kinesiology. It has the most amazing results and by changing your vibration you really can change your life.

I know of many cases using vibrational/energy healing where ill health has been eradicated!

We need to understand this vibrational stuff... 'cause it works!

Here is another simple technique to raise your vibration that I found very helpful:

Sit comfortably and close your eyes. Make sure you are not disturbed, and for the next 10 minutes say the word 'happiness' to yourself over and over, slowly and with feeling.

Feel the vibration of that word permeating your cells. Feel it moving through your mind and body, filling you up with the emotion of happiness. Do this for a week, at least 10 minutes a day (more if you have the time), and see if you feel happier.

You can do the same for peace, joy, love, abundance, etc. All of those wonderful qualities that you would like to increase so that they may enhance your life.

You may find that you say it during the day, while driving or walking around, whenever you like... the vibration of the word "happiness" will make you *feel* happy. Once you feel happy, you have raised your vibration and can now look at other qualities you wish to expand in your life.

Feeling happy is a pretty good place to start.

And happiness raises your vibration!

Remember, the inner work never ends; you are constantly evolving into your higher self towards endless levels of growth.

Wishing you all love, joy and laughter on your journey.

Anara   The Wake-Up Artist

Who is Anara?

Anara aka Linda Penny is a Vibrational Healer and Teacher.

I was given the name 'Anara' during the Harmonic Convergence in August 1987 through a meditation. This was a time when the planets in our solar system aligned in a way that hadn't occurred for a very long time, and created a more harmonic flow of positive energy to our planet and all who inhabit her.

It is only in the last few years that I have been guided to start using this name.

I'm passionate about healing and teaching, and have worked as Linda Penny for over 30 years in the UK, America and Asia. I'm a qualified Kinesiologist, Sound Healer and Reiki Master, and also work in the Quantum field.

I see clients both online and in person and am currently based in the UK.

My mission is to help as many people as possible.... to wake them up to their own magnificence, and teach them tools and techniques to achieve the next best version of themselves.

That is the purpose of this little book... enjoy!

Anara

Contact: Anara123@protonmail.com
Website: www.lindapenny.com

Lightning Source UK Ltd.
Milton Keynes UK
UKHW022025280922
409606UK00005B/155

9 781914 447556